What Our Readers Have Said...

Applicability

"These books are great tools that should be used as guidelines for our everyday supervisory practices. You need to take the time to do a short self-evaluation when reading them."

•

"The things and problems we deal with everyday are discussed in these books."

•

Convenience

"I like this because I can take them with me to read at a convenient time. I feel the little time I have to spend in the office is best use on activities that directly relate to revenue opportunities. I like the short amount of time it takes to keep up with these."

•

"I just read each book, and then file it for future reference."

•

"I like the fact that the format allows the books to be reviewed as time permits. All work has been conducted on personal, evening/weekend time."

•

Challenge

"My thought is that the real value of these books comes into effect when doing the action plans."

•

"The challenge when I think a specific topic does not apply is to find a way to make it apply."

•

Clarity

"Short and sweet. These books are easy to comprehend."

•

"These books are very easy to read and clearly outlined."

•

"Easy to use, understand, and reference if needed."

•

Relevance

"I have enjoyed reading these books. They are relevant to today's work environment and the ongoing change in the way we manage our workforce."

•

"I believe the contents of the Pinpoint series are excellent. It causes one to reflect on the daily dynamics in working with oneself as well as with management and peers."

•

"I do feel that these books have been very helpful to me at my job."

•

"I do enjoy reading each of theses books and it gives some real thought to its instruction."

•

Productively Managing Your Time

Pinpoint Customer Service Skill Development Training Series

TIMOTHY F. BEDNARZ

MAJORIUM
BUSINESS PRESS

Pinpoint Customer Service Skill Development Training Series
"Productively Managing Your Time"
Timothy F. Bednarz

Graphic design: Monika Pawlak

Majorium Business Press
2025 Main Street
Stevens Point, WI 54481
715.342.1018 • 800.654.4935

ISBN 978-1-882181-66-7

Printed in the United States of America

Introduction

The Pinpoint Customer Service Skill Development Training Series is designed for targeted training and education regarding increased improvement in a specific skill or competency.

Each book within this series is designed to be easy to use, understand and apply to your job. It can be used as a basis for training individuals, as a discussion guide or as a personal training tool.

Each chapter within this book discusses a specific concept. When you have completed all eight chapters you should have a 360º perspective of the topic.

Additionally, each chapter is divided into specific sections:

- The first section provides you with an overview of the topic
- The Implications section discusses why the concept is important, and why it is important to learn and apply.
- The Strategies, Tips & Techniques to Apply section teaches how to use and apply the particular concept to your work.
- The Points to Ponder section gives you something to think about or to be discussed with a group setting. These are questions not meant to be immediately answered, but to be pondered over time.
- The Training Activity section provides you with the tools to transfer what you have learned to your job. It is designed to help create an action plan to effectively apply the concept.

Each of the topics in this series is time-tested and proven in the marketplace. They have been used by thousands of employees as training tools. Many of the users have commented that what made these books valuable, was the ability to refer to them when a problem surfaced. They indicated that they remembered reading about the exact problem. They referred back to these books and found an appropriate solution.

You will find them equally valuable as a resource in your professional development library.

Table of Contents

LEARNING OBJECTIVES:

- To manage their time and activities.
- To keep their lives organized and uncluttered.
- How to manage the demands place upon their lives.
- Effective decision-making techniques.

1

Getting the Most out of the Workday

Individuals are feeling increasingly squeezed for time often at the expense of rest, recreation and relationships. By attempting to do too much with too little time, they risk overworking themselves. The constant overloading of their work capacities only leads to frustration, anxiety and fatigue.

IMPLICATIONS — WHAT THIS MEANS TO YOU

The "to-do" list is a common time management mechanism used by many in the business world. The more people need to do, the more pressure they feel. This is where the to-do list is helpful for organizing and prioritizing their activities. Unfortunately, by planning and filling every minute and second of their workday without careful consideration to interruptions, emergencies and meetings that occur in most business-related environments, many people fall short in applying this simple time management tool effectively and efficiently.

Most customer service representatives fail to account for the unplanned activities and events that surface during most business days. Additionally, most are unrealistic about their own capabilities and the time required to accomplish specific tasks within the day. Rather than devising a to-do list, they tend to create a "wish list" that invites frustration and fatigue at the end of the day.

STRATEGIES, TIPS & TECHNIQUES TO APPLY

It is important for individuals to create realistic to-do lists that reflect an objective assessment of their capacities and capabilities, and therefore, goals to be accomplished in realistic time frames. Several techniques can be applied that allow individuals to create a healthy and realistic time management tool for themselves. They include:

Limit Entries

The ability of individuals to limit the number of entries that they can realistically accomplish in a normal business day is fundamental to successful time management. If individuals understand what can be achieved and accomplished during a normal day, then everything else will fall into place where time management is concerned. Therefore, it is imperative that individuals be realistic about the expectations and time required to fill their business workdays. They should understand that their to-do list should help them get organized, stay on track, and accomplish the day's jobs and tasks assigned. Many find that fewer items on their list allows them the freedom to accomplish more during their business workdays.

Breathing Room

Many people have the tendency to plan their activities and tasks to a precise moment in time. They fall short in understanding how hindering this practice can be. To become more efficient, one technique is to overestimate the time scheduled for specific meetings, projects and tasks. This practice allows individuals to incorporate breathing room into their daily work schedules.

Form a Proper Mindset

A realistic development of a time management system for an individual requires the proper mindset. Too many individuals fill their schedules with unnecessary memos, tasks, calls and meetings, while continually feeling pressured with a sense of urgency to complete them before the end of every business working day. Individuals must prioritize work time and tasks in a manner best reflecting their importance and impact. With the proper mindset, many memos, tasks, calls and meetings can be eliminated that, if missed, would have no impact. With the proper mindset and the ability to eliminate unnecessary tasks and assignments, individuals can free up time and relieve much of the pressure they would otherwise feel.

Flexibility

Many time management tools such as day planners and palm pilots are essentially fancy to-do lists. Many individuals employ such tools in their daily work activities, attempting to fit their activities into a fairly rigid format. The key to effective time management is to find a format flexible enough to be effective and efficient. Individuals must have the ability to change and depart from their schedules. Therefore, it is necessary to create a format that comfortably fits individual work needs, rather than individuals trying to fit themselves into a pre-established and rigid format.

Prioritize

The main purpose of a time management system is to assure that the most important tasks get successfully completed during the business day. However, individuals should vary the pace, alternating difficult and easy tasks. A variation and change in activities maintains freshness and allows individuals to accomplish more during the course of their business day.

Smaller Steps

Many tasks and assignments confronting individuals can be overwhelming due to their size and complexity. Individuals are better served by breaking tasks down into smaller steps and spreading them out over several time periods, rather than concentrating on one time period to complete a large and overwhelming task or assignment. This allows individuals to be more effective and productive in the accomplishment of their goals and objectives.

Schedule Breaks

Many individuals schedule their time so tightly that they fail to create break and rest periods for themselves during the course of the day. Rests maintain a steady and efficient work pace; however, many fail to schedule them into their daily planning activities.

Break Down Long-Term Goals

Many to-do lists and time management systems tend to be tactical in nature, focusing on the day-to-day activities that must be accomplished. However, it is important for individuals to break down their long-term goals and subsequently schedule the necessary related activities within their daily schedules. By breaking down long-term goals into smaller, more easily achieved steps, individuals will find that they will accomplish far more over shorter periods of time in order to meet their overall goals and objectives for the year.

Increase Overall Productivity

Many become enslaved to their to-do lists and time management systems, but should understand that these devices are merely tools. The purpose of a good time management system is to increase overall productivity, not enslave individuals to the accomplishment of specific tasks and assignments.

Individuals should be ready to abandon their to-do list if specific opportunities present themselves that offer greater benefits than the daily tasks required of them. Additionally, individuals should view a to-do list as a suggestion of what to do with their time, rather than as absolute directives or edicts.

POINTS TO PONDER — SOMETHING TO THINK ABOUT

1. How rigidly do you plan your time, tasks and assignments for a specific day?
2. Do you find yourself enslaved to your to-do list or time management system?

TRAINING ACTIVITY — APPLICATION & ACTION PLAN

1. Review your daily activities and compare them to your daily or normal to-do list.
2. Allow flexibility and realistic time goals to govern your to-do list or time management system.
3. Revise your daily time management system to make realistic adjustments that better reflect your ability to adequately complete tasks.
4. Do this on a daily basis for a minimum of 30 days in order to create a habit and a more productive system to work within.

2

Principles of Moment Management

Many individuals focus on the big picture of how they invest their time, and carefully plan major demands while ignoring minor commitments that waste a great deal of their time during each business day. However, it is the minor time commitments that often have individuals spinning their wheels: they do things they do not want or need to do, which often means they do nothing at all as they patiently wait for something larger to happen.

IMPLICATIONS – WHAT THIS MEANS TO YOU

While many individuals will carefully plan out their major assignments and responsibilities for the day and the necessary time required to fulfill them, they fail to realize how much time is wasted by unplanned minor tasks and interruptions. In many business situations individuals can feel out of control because time is not theirs to manage, but is often dictated by others' schedules and priorities, unnecessary meetings, interruptions, demands and requests. From a time management standpoint, it is important for individuals to take control of the countless minutes that are wasted in every business day. Doing so will add precious hours to their personal schedules.

People make countless choices and numerous decisions every day that ultimately impact the amount of time they invest in them. Most decisions are made without consideration for the accompanying time commitment required. It is important for individuals to understand that they have conscious choices to make and each one of them has particular consequences in terms of their initial time investment.

STRATEGIES, TIPS & TECHNIQUES TO APPLY

The numerous choices individuals make during the day begin with how much time they want to spend before waking up and the route they should take to work. They include intricate and complex startup rituals to get individuals "warmed up" before beginning their jobs, and the choices go on from there. Individuals must understand that it is the management of the countless moments during each day that is important, not the management of hours. This can be accomplished by utilizing the following steps:

Decision

The mistake many individuals make when facing countless daily choices is that they waste time analyzing and agonizing over them. While this might be important for critical life and business decisions, many of the countless others made during the day are of little or no consequence. Yet, individuals tend to take precious time to ponder and worry over when to do things, and how to do them.

When encountering a particular choice, it is important to read the situation and evaluate the various options available. A simple decision might include hitting the snooze button when the alarm clock goes off: some individuals might worry that they need to get a fast start, but would like a few minutes more of sleep. They agonize over a decision that has little or no consequence on their day. Yet this simple decision is reflective of the countless choices individuals must make during the day. From a time management perspective, it is important to become decisive and make quick decisions regarding all necessary choices.

Review Options

Once individuals adequately read their situations and determine the options available, they should quickly review each one according to their impact. Individuals often waste time worrying over or second-guessing smaller decisions. In some instances, they can become paralyzed with a simple decision, not fully realizing that the choice is inconsequential. For example, one can spend a great deal of time reviewing the menu items at lunch and to decide what they are going to eat. Rather than make a quick choice, they become overwhelmed with the multitude of options. The ultimate consequence of their decision is meaningless, but they still spend a great deal of time deliberating. Even though this may seem minor, it is a practical example of how individuals often waste time during the day that ultimately affects their productivity and output.

Instant Response

Individuals must learn to respond with quick and decisive action without second-guessing themselves or worrying about subsequent remorse over their decisions. It is far better to make quick decisions and correct them later if pertinent information becomes available. Too often individuals are fearful of making wrong choices, and because of it, devote a great deal of time to them. While this is important in certain types of decisions, most made in the course of a day are not so life threatening that they demand a great deal of time to ponder and consider. When individuals understand that the time invested in decision making is often wasted, they can recoup many hours over the course of a week and apply it to far more productive pursuits.

POINTS TO PONDER — SOMETHING TO THINK ABOUT

1. Do you find yourself paralyzed over simple and minor decisions?
2. How quickly do you tend to make decisions and choices over the course of a normal day?

TRAINING ACTIVITY – APPLICATION & ACTION PLAN

Determine how many decisions you make in a day. Begin from the time you wake up and follow them through the time you get off from work. If you wish, include ones that relate to your work-at-home routine.

1. On a predetermined morning, carry a notepad and pencil with you to work. Begin to jot down the decisions you make throughout the day. Force yourself to be conscious of all the choices you make.
2. Review your list and check off specific choices from your routine that appear to be wasteful of time. Modify or delete them.
3. Repeat this activity for 30 days until it becomes a habit.

3

Getting a Jump Start on the Day

Most individuals suffer from some form of work aversion. This natural tendency makes getting started the hardest part of any job. While most individuals do not necessarily loathe their jobs, most would prefer to do something else. Time-consuming startup rituals at the beginning of the day often invite procrastination, which leads to a lack of overall productivity.

IMPLICATIONS – WHAT THIS MEANS TO YOU

Startup rituals might include such things as organizing papers, straightening the desktop, going over the day's activities, getting coffee, preparing a workplace for work, or developing a "to-do" list of tasks and assignments. While some of these activities actually help prepare for the day, most are subconsciously done to postpone the inevitable necessity of getting down to work.

If customer service representatives find themselves stalling, puttering, idling or starting various activities slowly throughout the day, there is a real need to evaluate their startup rituals in order to eliminate ones that waste time and sap productivity. If they don't, they will be continually pressed for time or unable to complete the essential tasks and responsibilities expected of them.

STRATEGIES, TIPS & TECHNIQUES TO APPLY

There are many ways individuals can get a jumpstart on their day that allows them to begin strongly and continue on at a consistent pace throughout it. These include:

Mental Preparation

The mental preparation to do a job properly should begin the night before. It is very helpful for individuals to create a positive visualization of how they will begin their day and to think of how to achieve their tasks and assignments in an easy, step-by-step manner. This mentally plants ideas of what they want to accomplish, allowing their subconscious to take over. The technique is used by professional athletes before an event or by actors before they go onto the stage. It allows them to mentally prepare to do their best.

Physical Preparation

Rather than completing multiple preparation activities at the beginning of the day, individuals should take time at the end of the workday to do them. Having files and information readily available the first thing in the morning can make customer service representatives more productive, which also saves significant amounts of time. When preparation is done before beginning the day, most activities can be started immediately.

Organization

Individuals should map out their day the night before, so they know exactly where to start and what to do when beginning work in the morning. Any planning and to-do lists should be prepared the day or evening before. Each day should begin with a specific plan that outlines the first hour or two in complete detail. Once they are on the job they can begin to implement the plan without the need to waste valuable time.

Starting Point

Individuals need to establish a starting point for their work activities. Big tasks that may seem overwhelming should be broken into smaller, more easily attainable steps. If individuals find it difficult to begin working in the morning, they should start with one task that is small and easy to accomplish. This allows them to set the pace for the day. Rather than procrastinate in selecting a particular task, it is important to decide quickly and decisively.

Regular Breaks

Many individuals tend to gain momentum while performing a particular small task or responsibility, and generally continue the momentum until it is completed. The key to completing more complex assignments is to stop and take a small break before fatigue sets in and an actual slowdown occurs. By stopping mid-task, individuals can ponder the next step to take, and are then motivated and energized to take it. This technique increases their productivity and is far better than being exhausted by the need to continually press on to accomplish more.

POINTS TO PONDER — SOMETHING TO THINK ABOUT

1. Do you have a complicated or complex startup ritual before the workday actually begins?
2. Do you have a tendency to procrastinate, or do you generally jumpstart your day?

TRAINING ACTIVITY — APPLICATION & ACTION PLAN

1. Identify the specific steps that you take to start your business day.
2. Outline these steps over a period of a week. Make sure to include all of the steps in your starting ritual.
3. After a week, review your startup ritual and determine which steps are

absolutely necessary to begin your day successfully.

4. Eliminate any unnecessary and time-wasting steps.
5. Continue this process for a minimum of 30 days until it becomes a habit.

4

Learning to Get Organized

It is not uncommon for individuals to be overwhelmed by the immensity of what has to be accomplished within their normal workday. Many see important goals and priorities get bumped off their daily schedule by numerous unforeseen occurrences, small emergencies and less important but necessary activities. It is a lack of an individual's ability to meet their goals and priorities that works to increase stress, frustration and anxiety.

IMPLICATIONS — WHAT THIS MEANS TO YOU

It is not uncommon for individuals to schedule general assignments on their workday to-do lists rather than specific tasks. When general assignments are scheduled, what needs to be done and when is not detailed, as opposed to scheduling a specific assignment step that can be set into a time frame reference.

Organizing and setting priorities must be as specific as possible. Otherwise they become too easy to ignore. Additionally, tasks should be comfortably scheduled for completion within a specific sequence and indicated time allotment.

STRATEGIES, TIPS & TECHNIQUES TO APPLY

There are specific techniques that individuals can use to organize their daily routine and activities. These include:

Breaking Long-Term Goals into Smaller, More Easily Obtainable Steps

Individuals will find that procrastination often results from a feeling of being overwhelmed by expected, assigned or mandated tasks and assignments. When individuals become overwhelmed, most are unable to see an exact starting point and because of it, waste vast amounts of time before beginning a project. They often fall short in thoroughly scheduling and planning the project through its completion, and as a result, appear to be spinning their wheels.

For maximum efficiency, it is essential to break projects down into smaller and easily obtainable steps. It is helpful to begin by planning backward, starting with the desired results or goals. Once this has been done, the steps required to obtain the targeted results should be determined then reviewed as to the additional steps or tasks needed to achieve their overall objectives. Once projects have been broken down into easily obtainable steps, individuals can develop a schedule or timeline to complete their projects and meet any necessary deadlines.

It is important to be conservative when planning time resources because sudden problems, delays, unplanned events and interruptions are constantly going to occur at various intervals. After scheduling and creating realistic project timelines, it is important for individuals to immediately begin completing all of them in sequence until the total project is completed.

Creating a Balanced Schedule

Everyone experiences unplanned events and emergencies that tend to interrupt their busy workday schedules. Because of it, individuals must learn to balance their time and schedules carefully. Time buffers and open plans allow individuals to build flexibility into their schedules and bring balance to the work process.

When individuals are faced with adding new items to a schedule, it is important to understand that something "has to give" in their plans. It is important for them to identify specifically what needs to or can realistically be dropped from their schedule when another item must be added.

When individuals are forced to drop an entry from their schedules, they must determine whether that particular item needs to be rescheduled or whether it can be eliminated altogether. They should question its necessity within the work schedule and determine its impact if it becomes eliminated.

Evaluation

As individuals learn to set goals and priorities, it is important that they evaluate their personal performance against them. This can be done by analyzing their daily performance and determining if the goals and priorities set for a specific day have been satisfactorily met. Individuals should observe whether daily goals and priorities remain unmet on a recurring basis and if so, transfer them to the next day's schedule. They must question the importance of their activities in determining whether these items can be dropped or realistically transferred. The major question to address is why they have not been accomplished if they are important.

Low Expectations

Individuals who are initially learning to organize and plan their activities should not expect immediate results. They should allow at least three to four weeks for planning techniques to become a habit. If during this period they tend to regress into old habits, it is important that they do not quit, as behavioral changes take time and practice to accomplish. However, when backsliding occurs, it is important to immediately begin applying the new planning activities once again.

POINTS TO PONDER — SOMETHING TO THINK ABOUT

1. Do you tend to schedule broader activities as opposed to specific tasks?
2. What do you tend to do when your priority setting and scheduling fails you?

TRAINING ACTIVITY — APPLICATION & ACTION PLAN

Identify a large and potentially overwhelming task that has been assigned to you.

1. Identify the desired result you wish to achieve.
2. Plan backwards from that result.
3. Identify specific steps to achieve the desired result.
4. Break each larger step down into smaller and more easily obtainable ones.
5. Schedule and timeline each subsequent task in order to meet specific deadlines.
6. Implement your plan immediately and follow through until it is completed.

5

Who Is Controlling Your Agenda

People often allow others to control their daily activities, regardless of what they are held accountable for and responsible to accomplish. Rather than saying "no," many allow others to intimidate them into taking part in insignificant conversations and activities that actively hinder progress toward accomplishing their personal goals.

IMPLICATIONS – WHAT THIS MEANS TO YOU

When people allow others to control their time, additional time must be found to accomplish the particular work and tasks assigned to them. Typically, when the day is filled with unimportant activities, additional time must be put in after working hours, at home or over the weekend. When this occurs, it is a clear indication of a poorly managed work life.

Customer service representatives must take control of both their life and time. They must develop the personal discipline and fortitude to ignore countless interruptions, unplanned events and meetings that tend to negatively interfere with their workday. They must learn to assume personal responsibility for their time and work-related activities.

STRATEGIES, TIPS & TECHNIQUES TO APPLY

There are several specific techniques that individuals can use to gain control over their personal agendas. These include:

Gather Purpose Before Committing

The most common unplanned interruption takes the form of the "Do you have a minute?" question. Most individuals are either intimidated or bullied into this interruption that often gets them off-focus. "Just a minute" can often easily become 20, 30 or more and create a situation in which they can lose momentum and their daily work plan.

Before people commit themselves to unplanned "minute-long" interruptions, they should ask what it is about and determine whether it should be considered urgent or important. If it is not, they should decline. If this is not possible, it is far better to schedule the interruption for a later time or date than to get pulled away and off-focus in the middle of something important.

Responsibility for Time

All people are responsible for their own time and how it is spent during the workday. They are also responsible for the results achieved through their work-related activities. Too often individuals allow others to set their agendas and how their daily time is spent. This results in additional pressure as deadlines loom and tasks remain unaccomplished. This in turn raises their stress, anxiety and frustration levels, compelling them to devote personal time to completing certain tasks that would otherwise have been completed during the normal workday. Individuals must learn to manage their time wisely by learning to say "no" to unplanned interruptions and low priority items.

Endless Meetings

One of the greatest interruptions to work schedules is the number of meetings individuals are expected to attend. Undoubtedly, there are meetings that cannot be avoided, or which are mandatory for all to attend. However, many meetings are discretionary. This is where individuals must take control and examine whether there is a real need to attend or create a meeting, especially in view of the fact that there are often other alternatives to accomplishing the same goal such as conference calls, webcasts, emails and simple memos.

Preserving Time Integrity

It is important that individuals maintain their time and priorities and not relinquish their workday. They have specific responsibilities that must be accomplished, and need to learn tactful ways to avoid countless interruptions, meetings and unplanned events that rob them of valuable time. It is important for individuals to maintain the integrity of their time and work schedules in order to perform critical tasks and meet specifically assigned deadlines.

Schedule Downtime

Individuals must actively schedule downtime just for themselves. This creates a buffer zone for the interruptions that are likely to occur during the day. Scheduled downtime can include time to:

- Do paperwork
- Initiate tasks rather than react to them
- Think
- Read
- Exercise
- Do nothing

By leaving open spaces and scheduling downtime, individuals create breathing room within their schedules that allows them to accommodate some of the interruptions they are likely to encounter during their business day.

POINTS TO PONDER — SOMETHING TO THINK ABOUT

1. Do you find that time is wasted by countless meetings and unplanned interruptions?
2. Are you afraid to say "no" when asked if you have a minute?

TRAINING ACTIVITY — APPLICATION & ACTION PLAN

Review your calendar for the past several weeks. Before doing so, make sure all the activities that you actually performed during a given business day are reflected within it.

1. Using colored marking pens, color-code your calendar as to events, interruptions, activities, etc.
2. Look for a dominant color to determine where your time is being spent.
3. Review all the colors to determine if there is a balance in how you spend your time.
4. Color-code your calendar in advance for specific events and activities that create a proper balance for yourself. When you run out of space in regard to a specific color, do not schedule another event or responsibility assigned to that color.

6

Does This Activity Move Me Forward?

While every individual should have a focus that advances him or her toward the overall accomplishment of their goals and objectives, many get bogged down in a myriad of daily meetings, phone calls and sundry activities. Rather than progress toward his or her goals, the individual's efforts seem to be on daily crises that always appear at the last moment, resulting in a complete loss of focus.

IMPLICATIONS – WHAT THIS MEANS TO YOU

Time is the one element in customer service—and in life—that can manage the service representative or the representative can manage. Managing it is something that can easily spin out of control, as the complexities of the job seem to take over the service representative's life. Without realizing it, because it happens slowly and incrementally, the service representative is controlled by time and events rather than effectively managing the one resource so essential to their success.

This is important for service representatives to understand and grasp, because over time, they can commit or get obligated to a number of tasks and activities that sap valuable time. This diminishes their personal effectiveness and productivity.

STRATEGIES, TIPS & TECHNIQUES TO APPLY

Every service representative should have a system or method of effectively managing his or her time and activities. Whether on the back of an envelope, with a Palm Pilot, or the variety of options in between, every customer service representative (and for that matter, every business person) needs to have a system that organizes, schedules and plans the various activities of the day. Since every service representative has their own unique style, the system should match that which they are most comfortable using, or they will not use it. The reality of it all is no matter what the service representative's preference and what he or she paid for it, it is ultimately a fancy "to-do" list.

Most customer service representatives use planners and planning systems because they are key to managing their time and activities. However, the one thing these systems cannot do is prioritize the service representative's daily activities. Few individuals will take the time to weigh the activities listed on whatever system they use.

Any planning system is useless without the essential step of priority setting. People may look important walking down the street with a cell phone stuck to their ear and a Filofax in their hands, but most waste much of their time on tasks and projects that don't advance them toward the successful accomplishment of their major goals. Consequently many service representatives spend time on things that have no real value or impact on their professional lives.

Every night or every week, whenever a service representative plans their activities, he or she should ask this simple question of every item on their calendar or agenda: "Does this activity advance me forward to the successful accomplishment of my major goals?" If the answer is negative, the service representative should immediately remove, delegate or cancel those activities that do not move them toward the accomplishment of their goals. This simple technique identifies the specific activities that are wasting the service representative's time and costing him or her money.

It should be noted that many activities are addictive and difficult to break away from. This is because it removes the façade that the service representative is busy. However, as being busy does not equate to effectiveness, the service representative must shift their activities to those that produce results and have a direct impact on the accomplishment of their goals.

POINTS TO PONDER — SOMETHING TO THINK ABOUT

1. What priorities control your activities?
2. Are the demands being placed upon you contributing or detracting from your personal success?

TRAINING ACTIVITY — APPLICATION & ACTION PLAN

Every night or week for the next 30 days, whenever you plan your activities, ask this simple question of every item on your calendar or agenda:

"Does this activity advance me forward to the successful accomplishment of my major goals?"

If the answer is negative, immediately remove, delegate or cancel those activities that do not move you ahead toward the accomplishment of your goals.

7

Controlling Clutter

It is easier for individuals to manage incoming mail and documents daily than to devote time in a pressing schedule to deal with the clutter and get organized on a periodic basis.

IMPLICATIONS – WHAT THIS MEANS TO YOU

Cluttered desktops and offices are common occurrences. Many people have "nesting" instincts that offer them comfort and reassurance when they surround themselves with familiar objects, letters, schedules etc. Some save documents, never knowing when they might need them. Others are simply afraid that if they cannot physically "see" something, or have whatever it is they feel they may need occasionally or regularly at their fingertips, it will be lost forever. Then there are those individuals who feel that clutter labels them as "creative and innovative" individuals. Whatever the reason, common office clutter saps time and energy.

The more organized individuals are, the more efficient and productive they become. It is important for them to schedule time to organize and clean the clutter in their offices on a daily basis in order to maintain their maximum efficiency.

STRATEGIES, TIPS & TECHNIQUES TO APPLY

Individuals should make it a habit to schedule time every day for handling incoming mail, memos and other paperwork that crosses their desk. Below are some techniques that can be used to help maintain daily organizational efficiency.

Toss Envelopes

Opened envelopes and their inserts create a great deal of clutter on the desktop. Individuals should toss envelopes immediately. If there is a need to save any particular addresses, they should be entered into an electronic or physical address book where they can readily be referenced. Another method is to clip the address from the envelope and attach it to the related document, and then file it accordingly.

Schedule Meetings and Appointments

Rather than accumulate meeting notices and memos, individuals should immediately detail them on a calendar. They should be inserted as to when these particular meetings or appointments are scheduled and what is needed to bring to them. Once this is done the initial documents should be thrown away.

Create Files

If individuals need to save a document and do not have a place for it, it is necessary for them to create a file, label it and then put it away.

Schedule

If paperwork and materials require sustained action and activity, individuals should use post-it notes to indicate what needs to be done and accomplished, and the deadline for it. They should then schedule the activity rather than putting it on a "to-do later" pile. In this way, the paperwork will be handled in an efficient and timely manner, and not be lost. This aids individuals in meeting their required task and overall assignment deadlines.

Peruse Newsletters and Periodicals

Many individuals are placed on routing lists for periodicals and newsletters. Many of these do not get read because of a lack of interest, or because individuals do not have the time to read through them. Rather than handling newsletters and periodicals and routing them to another person, it is better for individuals to eliminate their names from specific routing lists. In this manner, these unread materials will not lay dormant on their desks, shelves or on top of their filing cabinets before remembering to send them along.

If individuals must read newsletters and periodicals, they should scan them, cut out or photocopy any articles of interest, and file them in a current reading folder for scheduled reading at a later time. In this way the unwanted accompanied materials can be immediately disposed of.

Identify Papers

One effective technique for eliminating unnecessary paperwork is to use colored "adhesive dots" on papers and materials that cannot be filed, thrown away, recycled or completed. Every time the paperwork or files are moved, read, transferred or handled, another dot should be added. This creates a visual testimony of the amount of time individuals are wasting on managing their clutter.

POINTS TO PONDER — SOMETHING TO THINK ABOUT

1. Do you feel excessive clutter hampers your performance and wastes your time? Why or why not?
2. How regularly do you take the time to control the clutter within your office or workspace?

TRAINING ACTIVITY – APPLICATION & ACTION PLAN

1. Schedule a daily block of time to handle your mail, paperwork and memos.
2. Specifically apply the colored dot technique detailed within this lesson.
3. Place a dot on papers that you cannot file, toss or recycle, and add another dot every time you handle them.
4. Determine how much time you have devoted to the repetitious handling of these "dotted" documents.

8

Maximizing Your Time Means Setting Priorities

One of the customer service representative's most commonly voiced complaints relates to the lack of time to perform their tasks and responsibilities during the typical business day. Most are able to recognize the obvious ways time is wasted. Yet, many are impervious to time wasters such as unrelated service tasks, numerous meetings, unproductive activities and assignments.

Customer service representatives who are able to recognize how their time is spent can take the first step in controlling and organizing it more effectively and efficiently.

IMPLICATIONS — WHAT THIS MEANS TO YOU

Customer service representatives who waste the least time have the most to gain. Good organization, including long- and short-range planning and priority setting, are absolutely necessary to eliminate time-wasting tasks. Hard work and preparation are essential. It is important to think about tomorrow, next week and into the future, while setting proper objectives and anticipating needs before they arise. Service representatives must further have the personal determination and discipline to work their plans and resist activities that do not advance their goals.

The first priority of all customer service representatives should be to achieve their goals and maximize their results and performance. During the normal course of business, it is too easy to become engaged in more unproductive activities that undermine these major priorities.

STRATEGIES, TIPS & TECHNIQUES TO APPLY

Effective personal management requires customer service representatives to evaluate their workloads on a daily basis and establish a prioritized list for each day. To be most effective, they should use the time when workloads are light to follow up, and organize their work, extra activities and work areas, to avoid cutting into productive times.

Some techniques service representatives can use to manage their time more effectively and efficiently in order to eliminate wasted effort include:

Goals and Objectives

Customer service representatives need to establish clear and concise goals and objectives and review them frequently. They must continually question whether a particular activity will move them closer to their goals and objectives. If it doesn't, they need to eliminate it. Where possible, they should organize their time into 15-minute periods. It is inadequate management to schedule a day's activities in one-hour blocks.

Meetings

Countless meetings can easily bog down customer service representatives. When meetings are continuous, many are compelled to arrive early at the office and stay late just to handle their phone messages, correspondence and emails. Service representatives must determine whether their presence is essential before agreeing to attend particular meetings. Unnecessary ones should be avoided, and where possible, other individuals should be assigned to attend on their behalf. When attendance at a meeting is mandatory, it should only be scheduled long enough to meet the essential objectives of the topic.

Delegation

Service representatives need to consider delegating many of the nonessential tasks that do not advance them toward the attainment of their goals and objectives. When and where possible, they should utilize other employees that may have lighter workloads or individuals within other departments who can help ease some of the task burdens in order to increase their overall effectiveness. In some cases, eliminating certain tasks altogether may be a possibility.

Prime Time

Service representatives need to use prime contact hours to manage and handle customer inquiries and complaints. Any non-customer related activity should be conducted during off hours. Prime contact time is when service representatives should be in front of their customers. Service representatives hinder themselves when they do other people's work for them, or waste time on non-customer related activities.

Use of Time Management Aids

Service representatives must use technology to increase their effectiveness. This includes the use of phone, mail, call management systems, and other management aids to make more productive use of their time. When possible, service representatives should send their dictation and notes to an assistant who can subsequently enter the information into the contact system. It can easily save up to an hour a day and half a day per week for working toward other goals and objectives.

POINTS TO PONDER — SOMETHING TO THINK ABOUT

1. How often do you analyze your time by using and reviewing a daily activity log?
2. Do you analyze and scrutinize your activities to assure that you're maximizing the best use of your time? Explain.

TRAINING ACTIVITY — APPLICATION & ACTION PLAN

1. Every night or every week, whenever you plan your activities, ask this simple question of every item on your calendar or agenda: "Does this activity advance me forward to the successful accomplishment of my major goals?"
2. Score each item on your calendar.
3. Remove, delegate or cancel those activities that do not move you forward. They're time wasters that only add to your frustration and your inability to achieve professional success.

About the Author

Timothy F. Bednarz, Ph.D. is CEO of the American Management Development Group, Inc. For over 20 years he has researched, designed and authored hundreds of learning and development programs used by Fortune 1000 companies.

He is also the author of *Great! What Makes Leaders Great. What They Did, How They Did It and What You Can Learn from It* (2011).

Speaking Availability

Timothy F. Bednarz, Ph.D. is available for speaking engagements for your next meeting or association event. He can be contacted at 800-654-4935 or by e-mail at timothy.bednarz@majorium.com.

Bulk Sales

Bulk sales of this book or any other titles available from Majorium Business Press. Inquiries can be directed to sales@majorium.com, or by phone at 800-6654-4935.

Quick Order Form

Fax orders: 715-342-1118. Send this form.

Telephone orders: Call 800-654-4935 toll-free. Have your credit card ready.

Email orders: sales@majorium.com

Postal orders: Majorium Business Press, 2025 Main Street, Stevens Point, WI 54481, USA.

Please send the following books:

____

____

____

____

Please send more FREE information on:

❑Catalog ❑Speaking/Seminars ❑Mailing Lists ❑Consulting

Name: ____________________________________

Address: ____________________________________

City: ____________________ State: _____ Zip: __________

Telephone: ____________________________________

Email address: __________________________________

Sales tax: Please add 5.5% for products shipped to Wisconsin addresses.

Shipping by air:

United States: $4.00 for first book and $2.00 for each additional product.

International: $9.00 for first book; $5.00 for each additional product (estimate).

Made in the USA
Monee, IL
08 November 2026

67380795R00026